CROFTON MIDDLE SCHOOL
MEDIA CENTER

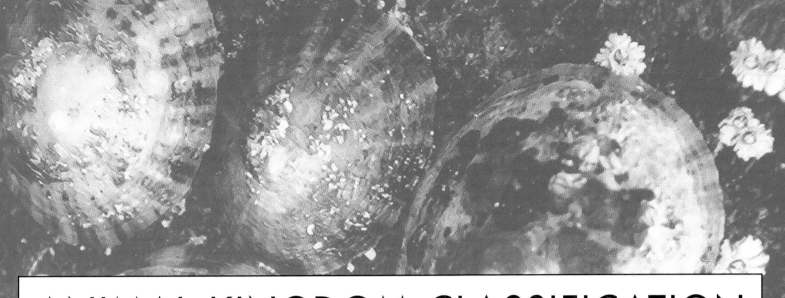

ANIMAL KINGDOM CLASSIFICATION

SNAILS, SHELLFISH & OTHER
MOLLUSKS

By Daniel Gilpin

Content Adviser: Timothy A. Pearce, Ph.D., Assistant Curator and Head,
Section of Mollusks, Carnegie Museum of Natural History

Science Adviser: Terrence E. Young Jr., M.Ed., M.L.S.,
Jefferson (Louisiana) Public School System

First published in the United States in 2006 by
Compass Point Books
3109 West 50th St., #115
Minneapolis, MN 55410

ANIMAL KINGDOM CLASSIFICATION–MOLLUSKS
was produced by

David West Children's Books
7 Princeton Court
55 Felsham Road
London SW15 1AZ

Designer: David West
Editors: Gail Bushnell, Anthony Wacholtz, Kate Newport
Page Production: James Mackey

Visit Compass Point Books on the Internet at
www.compasspointbooks.com
or e-mail your request to
custserv@compasspointbooks.com

Library of Congress Cataloging-in-Publication Data
Gilpin, Daniel.
  Snails, shellfish & other mollusks / by Daniel Gilpin.
    p. cm.—(Animal kingdom classification)
  Includes bibliographical references.
  ISBN 0-7565-1613-7 (hard cover)
  1. Mollusks—Juvenile literature. 2. Snails—Juvenile literature. 3. Shellfish—Juvenile literature. I. Title: Snails, shellfish, and other mollusks. II. Title. III. Series.
    QL405.2.G55 2006
    594—dc22   2005029182

PHOTO CREDITS:
Abbreviations: t-top, m-middle, b-bottom, r-right, l-left, c-center.

Pages 8t, Olaf Ziehe, 8m, Steve McWilliam, 8c, Rachel Blaser; 8-9b, G. Wenz, OAR/National Undersea Research Program (NURP); Caribbean Marine Research Center , 9br, Dan Schmitt; 11t, Timothy Large; 12t, Gert Bukacek, 12b, Dan Schmitt, 12r, Oxford Scientific; 13t, Dan Schmitt; 15t, Bruce Stephens; 16t, 16l, Oxford Scientific; 17b, Oxford Scientific; 18b, Paul Topp; 19t, 19b, Oxford Scientific; 20t, Willem Dijkstra, 20b, Paul Rogers; 21l, 21t, 21b, Oxford Scientific; 22t, Oxford Scientific; 23t, Oxford Scientific, 23l, Kip Evans NOAA, 23r, NOAA; 24l, U.S. Fish and Wildlife Service, 24r, Oxford Scientific; 25l, 25r, Oxford Scientific; 26t, Steve McWilliam, 26m, Jeffrey McDonald; 27t, 27b, Oxford Scientific; 28l, Oxford Scientific; 30t, Oxford Scientific; 31l, U.S. Fish and Wildlife Service Photo; 32l, L. Levin, 32r, Oxford Scientific; 33t, Oxford Scientific; 35t, 35l, Oxford Scientific; 36, Oxford Scientific; 37t, 37r, Oxford Scientific; 38l, Oxford Scientific, 38r, Paul Rogers; 39l, 39r, Oxford Scientific; 40t, 40b, Oxford Scientific; 41t, T. Schaff, OAR/National Undersea Research Program (NURP); North Carolina State University, 41b, Oxford Scientific; 42t, NOAA National Estuarine Research, 42bl, ravi tahilramani, 42br, Dr. Roger Mann, VIMS; 43tl, Andrei Tchernov, 43tr, 43b, Oxford Scientific

Every effort has been made to contact copyright holders of any material reproduced in this book. Any omissions will be rectified in subsequent printings if notice is given to the publishers.

With special thanks to the models: Felix Blom, Tucker Bryant, and Margaux Monfared.

Front cover: Nautilus
Opposite: Snail

ANIMAL KINGDOM CLASSIFICATION

NAILS, SHELLFISH & OTHER MOLLUSKS

Daniel Gilpin

COMPASS POINT BOOKS MINNEAPOLIS, MINNESOTA

TABLE OF CONTENTS

INTRODUCTION

With more than 100,000 species known to science, mollusks make up a huge and varied animal group. The most familiar mollusks—slugs and snails—are land-living animals, but the vast majority of this group spend their lives in the sea.

Far more sea creatures are mollusks than most people realize. Along with shellfish they include more complex animals, the largest and most intelligent of all being the cuttlefish, octopuses, and squid.

In marine environments, the mollusks are hugely successful, living from the tropics to cold polar waters. They inhabit the seabed, open waters, and ocean surface, and can also be found living on most of the world's shores. Slugs and snails have colonized most of the world's land habitats. They are most often seen where it is damp and the air is humid. Elsewhere, they avoid direct sunlight but can emerge at night in huge numbers when it rains.

BRIGHT AND BEAUTIFUL

Some mollusks are incredibly colorful. Many sea slugs use color and bold patterns to warn other animals to stay away. Although only some are poisonous, they all bristle with hidden defenses. Some varieties can transfer stinging cells into the skin of the corals and sea anemones on which they feed.

MOLLUSK TYPES

SNAIL

Mollusks make up the most varied of all animal groups. Their soft, unsegmented bodies have let them evolve into a huge range of forms, allowing them to exploit almost all of the world's habitats.

CLASS ACTS

SLUG

Scientists usually group mollusks into seven groups, each with its own class in the animal classification system. By far the largest class, with more than 35,000 species, is the one that contains slugs, snails, limpets, and their relatives. These are known as gastropods, which is Latin for "stomach foot." All gastropods have a single, large "foot," which they use to move. The second biggest class, with just over 15,000 species, contains the bivalves, which have paired, hinged shells. Octopuses, squid, and cuttlefish have their own class named Cephalopoda. Other mollusk classes contain the chitons, monoplacophorans, tusk shells, and aplacophorans.

SCALLOP

SQUID

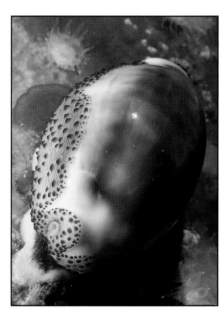

COWRIE

OCTOPUS

CONCH BED

Like land slugs and snails, sea slugs are gastropods, traveling by means of a single, large "foot." Unlike most of their land cousins, these creatures are carnivores, feeding on corals and other creatures that cannot get away. Sea slugs are very common in tropical waters, but some species are found nearer the poles. Most are no larger than a human finger, but a few can grow to more than 1 foot (30 cm) long.

Sea slugs do not have lungs but breathe through feathery gills on their backs.

Although some sea slugs stand out, others are well-camouflaged, matching the colors of the corals on which they live and feed.

THE MOLLUSCAN BODY

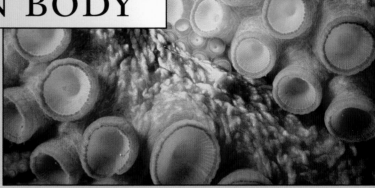

Mollusks come in a huge range of shapes and sizes, but all have variations of the same basic body plan. Mollusks are invertebrates, and they all possess highly developed blood and nervous systems.

SHELLS, FEET, AND TENTACLES

Mollusk bodies are soft and flexible—the word *mollusk* comes from the Latin for "soft bodied." Most mollusks have shells, which grow from an outer layer of flesh called the mantle. Mollusk shells are made from the mineral calcium carbonate.

Unlike those of many worms, mollusk bodies are not segmented but form a single unit, usually with a head at one end. Most have a single foot but cephalopods have lost this and have tentacles instead.

GETTING A GRIP

The tentacles of cephalopods are lined with suckers to grab prey and other objects. Squid suckers have sharp toothlike projections around the edges. Those of octopuses (above) do not.

GASTROPODS

The garden snail is a typical gastropod, with a large foot, a rasping "tongue" called a radula, and a big, external shell. Most of its organs are contained inside the shell. It can pull the rest of its body in for protection when danger threatens. In land slugs, the shell has become internalized, while in sea slugs it has been lost altogether.

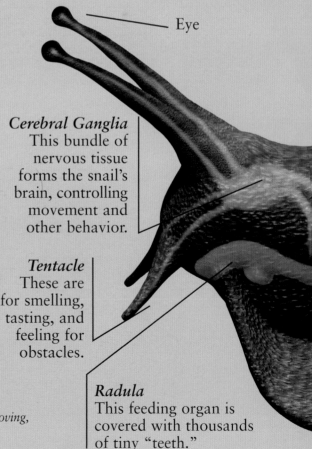

— Eye

Cerebral Ganglia
This bundle of nervous tissue forms the snail's brain, controlling movement and other behavior.

Tentacle
These are for smelling, tasting, and feeling for obstacles.

Radula
This feeding organ is covered with thousands of tiny "teeth."

BIVALVES

These filter-feeding mollusks are almost completely surrounded by their twin shells. The foot is used for digging or clinging to rock.

Gill

Shell

Siphon   Foot

CEPHALOPODS

The largest and most complex of all invertebrates, cephalopods are fast-moving, active hunters that swim in open water.

Shell

Feeding Arm

Radula

Pen

LUNGS OR GILLS?

Slugs breathe through a hole in their mantle.

The first mollusks evolved in the sea. They took the oxygen they needed from the water using gills, just as their aquatic descendants do today. Mollusk gills consist of filaments covered with tiny hairlike structures called cilia. These cilia beat rhythmically, moving old water, with the oxygen removed from it, off the filaments and drawing new, oxygen-rich water onto them. Some mollusks take in oxygen directly through their mantles. In slugs and snails, part of the mantle became internal and evolved into a lung.

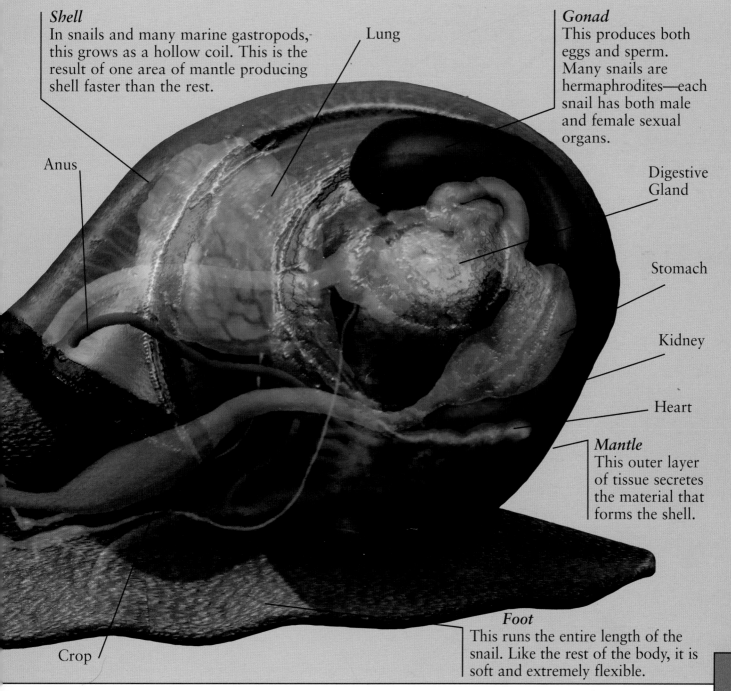

Shell
In snails and many marine gastropods, this grows as a hollow coil. This is the result of one area of mantle producing shell faster than the rest.

Lung

Anus

Gonad
This produces both eggs and sperm. Many snails are hermaphrodites—each snail has both male and female sexual organs.

Digestive Gland

Stomach

Kidney

Heart

Mantle
This outer layer of tissue secretes the material that forms the shell.

Foot
This runs the entire length of the snail. Like the rest of the body, it is soft and extremely flexible.

Crop

WHERE MOLLUSKS LIVE

Mollusks have colonized most of the Earth. They are found throughout the oceans, which cover almost three quarters of the planet's surface, and are common in freshwater, as well as many land habitats.

THE NEED FOR WATER

For mollusks to be active, it has to be damp. Land-living slugs and snails are common in the tropics and in most temperate countries, but they are almost completely absent from dry habitats like deserts. As well as moisture, these creatures need food. Most land slugs and snails are vegetarians—if plants are scarce, so are they.

Ponds, lakes, and rivers are havens for mollusks, particularly bivalves and gastropods. Most freshwater mollusks have gills, but a few pond snails breathe air.

MOBILE HOME
Snails and slugs find it hard to live in freezing temperatures. Although they are common in many parts of the world, they do not inhabit polar regions.

SEABED SKULKERS
Sea slugs live on the ocean floor. Most inhabit shallow tropical waters and are particularly common around coral reefs.

JUST UNDER THE SURFACE
The violet sea snail creates mucus bubbles that harden soon after being formed. It uses its bubble raft to float in search of creatures such as the Portuguese man-of-war, on which it feeds.

OCEAN DWELLERS

The majority of mollusks live in the sea. Five of the seven classes (chitons, tusk shells, cephalopods, monoplacophs, and aplacophs) are found nowhere else. Mollusks inhabit virtually every part of the ocean, feeding on everything from algae to fish. Some live in the sediment on the bottom, while others cling to rocks or glide over reefs. Still more swim through the open ocean and lurk in the dark depths. As land creatures ourselves, it is hard to imagine how many there are. To get an idea, count the seashells next time you visit a beach.

IN OPEN WATER

Cephalopods such as this reef squid are excellent swimmers, able to move slowly, speed along, and even hover in one spot. Unlike octopuses and most cuttlefish, squid often form shoals, or large groups, for protection from predators. Some species live in shallow waters and others at great depths.

BETWEEN THE TIDES

Many mollusks spend their adult lives along rocky shores. Some live fixed to one spot, filtering the water for tiny particles of food. Others move about, grazing algae from the rocks. When the tide goes out, all of these mollusks risk drying out in the air. Bivalves, such as mussels, clamp their shells tightly shut, while gastropods, such as limpets, pull themselves tight against the rocks.

When the tide goes out, mussels close their shells in order to keep their bodies moist.

MOLLUSK EVOLUTION

Although mollusks are common now, they were once even more abundant. Before the evolution of fish, they ruled the oceans, making up most of the world's top predators as well as many of the species farther down the food chain.

EARLY ANCESTORS

The first mollusks appeared in the oceans around 550 million years ago. The oldest known mollusk fossils include monoplacophorans that still have relatives alive today. Alongside them lived the rostroconchs that are now extinct. Rostroconchs had folded shells that almost completely enclosed their bodies and are thought by some scientists to be the ancestors of today's bivalves.

MODERN MOLLUSKS APPEAR

Around 500 million years ago, all of the mollusk classes we know today had appeared. Some of the creatures they contained were quite different from modern mollusks, but others looked very similar to present-day sea creatures. The first land snails appeared around 315 million years ago. Around the same time, bivalves first began moving into freshwater habitats.

ANCIENT OCEAN

Around 500 million years ago, the first, primitive fish began to appear in an ocean world already filled with mollusks. Early ammonites ① were among the most fearsome predators, along with the straight-shelled nautilus ②.

FOSSIL SCALLOP

Bivalves and other shelled mollusks made good fossils. However, fossils of soft-bodied mollusks, such as sea slugs, are extremely rare.

1

COILED COUSINS

When dinosaurs were roaming the land, ammonites were among the most common animals in the sea. Cousins of today's squid and octopuses, they hunted fish and other open-water creatures. Some ammonites were little bigger than a coin, but others were huge, growing to the size of truck tires.

Ammonites disappeared 65 million years ago. They were wiped out at the same time as the dinosaurs.

HOW MOLLUSKS MOVE

Slugs and snails are famous for moving slowly—we have all heard the saying "to move at a snail's pace." Some mollusks, however, can move pretty quickly. Cephalopods, such as squid, even have jet propulsion.

SLOW BUT SURE
Gastropods move by means of a muscular foot, which covers the entire underside of the body. The foot is stretched out by an increase in blood pressure in its tissues, combined with the use of powerful muscles. It is contracted by muscle action alone. In order to move, the gastropod ripples the muscles on the base of its foot, sending waves of motion from the rear to the front. Movement is helped by mucus secreted from the foot and left behind the animal as a slimy trail.

LITTLE SNAPPERS

Unusual for bivalves, scallops can swim. They do this by snapping their shells shut and forcing water jets out of the hinge side.

UP AND DOWN
Some bivalve mollusks spend their lives in mud or sand, removing food particles from the water above. Like gastropods, many of these creatures have a muscular foot, but it is used for burrowing rather than traveling over flat surfaces. In most species, the foot is extended outward into the sediment, inflated to form an anchor, then contracted to pull the shell and the rest of the bivalve toward it.

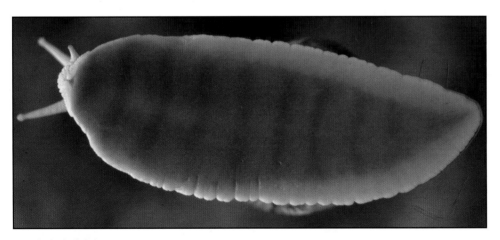

BIG FOOT

Like most other gastropods, the Roman snail ripples the muscles on the underside of its foot to move itself slowly along.

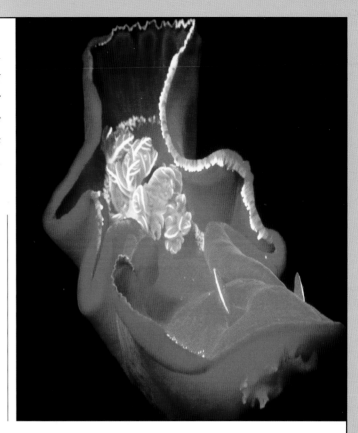

SWIMMERS

A few gastropods and bivalves can swim, usually as a means of escape. The masters of molluscan swimming are the cephalopods. They move through the water with an ease matched only by marine mammals and fish.

JET POWERED

Octopuses and other cephalopods use jets of water to get around. They move by sucking water into the space between the mantle and the rest of the body, then squirting it out at high pressure to send themselves shooting off in the opposite direction. By varying the force with which they squirt the water out, they are able to adjust their speed. They also move slowly by using their tentacles.

Cephalopods, like this lesser octopus, trail their tentacles as they swim along.

MOLLUSK SENSES

All mollusks experience the world through touch. Many types can also see, and the majority have other senses that are linked to taste and smell.

EYES AND FEELERS

Slugs and snails have four stalks sticking out from their heads. The top two stalks bear eyes while the bottom two are for smell and taste.

FEELING THE WAY

Most mollusks react instinctively to vibration. The thud of a footstep, for instance, quickly sends a snail into its shell. Touch is most important to mollusks that live in darkness, such as those that burrow or live in the deep sea. Some gastropods have feelers to help enhance their sense of touch.

MOLLUSK VISION

Eyesight is more important to some mollusks than others. For most gastropods and bivalves it is mainly an extra sense to help them avoid predators. Shadows cast by larger animals cause a similar reaction to heavy vibrations. Cephalopods, however, have extremely well-developed eyes. As predators themselves, good eyesight is very useful in helping them to detect prey.

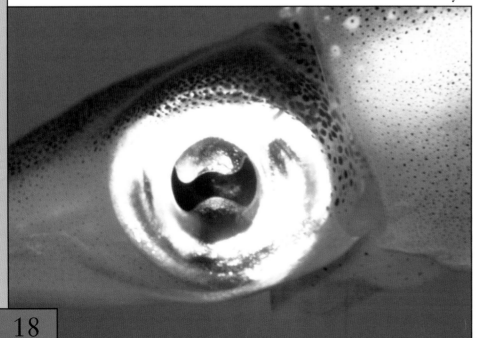

SLIT-SHAPED PUPIL

Cephalopod eyes are unusual because instead of a lens, they have a curved mirror (like a reflector telescope). They can change the curvature of the mirror to focus the image.

GIANT EYES

The world's biggest eyes belong to a mollusk. The giant squid, which lives and hunts in the deep ocean, has eyes the size of saucers, enabling it to see the movement of prey in even the faintest light. Several other large species of squid have big eyes for exactly the same reason. Like our own eyes, they have a single lens to focus light.

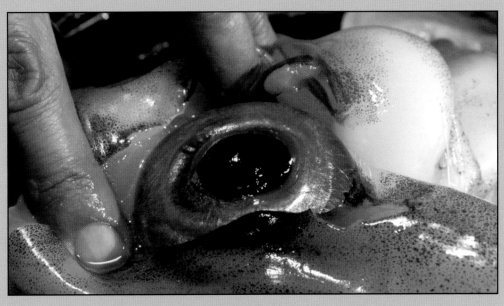

The Humboldt squid can be 18 feet (5.5 meters) long and has huge eyes.

CHEMICAL SENSES

Chemical sense is probably the most important sense to most mollusks. By picking up chemical signals, or flavors, mollusks, such as scallops, can identify and avoid predators. Other gastropods use taste to find their way around. As the tide starts to go out, limpets use taste to follow the trail of their own mucus back to their usual position on the rocks. Finding this exact spot is important for the shell to fit tightly and to make sure no water escapes.

Bivalve larvae also pick up chemical signals. These are given off by the adults to lead larvae to safe places to settle.

BEADY EYES

Scallops have dozens of simple eyes ranged along the inside edges of their shells. If these detect danger, the two shells snap shut to protect the animal's soft body tissues.

19

FOOD AND FEEDING

As a group, mollusks feed upon just about everything. Some eat plants and others hunt. Many eat tiny particles sifted from their surroundings.

EATING GREENS

Many gastropods are vegetarians, feeding on green matter. The majority of slugs and snails eat plants, while their marine cousins, limpets and winkles, feed on algae. Some gastropods, such as the common whelk, eat the remains of dead animals, and a few species hunt.

SALAD MUNCHER

Like most land mollusks, the garden snail eats leaves. A few snails, however, are carnivorous. Most eat other mollusks, worms, and insect larvae. One, the rosy wolf snail, hunts down and kills other varieties of snail, including giant African land snails.

SUSPENSION FEEDERS

Suspension feeders remove food particles from the water. Many bivalves and some gastropods survive in this way. The food they eat includes plankton—tiny floating animals and algae—as well as dead matter. Suspension-feeding mollusks suck water in through a tube called a siphon. Food sticks to mucus on their feathery gills and is transported to the mouth by tiny, beating hairlike structures called cilia.

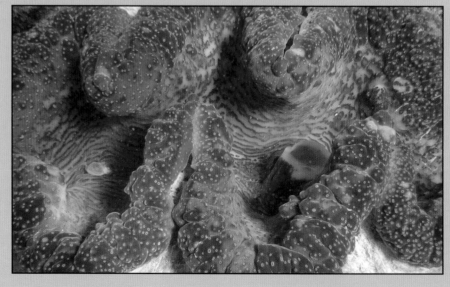

Suspension feeders, like clams, don't need to move to find food.

ROUGH TONGUE

Many mollusks have a radula, which they use to rasp away at food. The surface of this tongue-like organ is covered with tiny "teeth," giving it the texture of a nail file. The individual teeth on a radula are too small to be seen. A conch's radula (left) are shown magnified many times.

MARINE CARNIVORES

Cephalopods are formidable predators. Squid and cuttlefish have two extra-long tentacles that they shoot out to grab their victims. Their keen eyesight helps them not only to find prey but also judge distances well, improving the accuracy of their attacks. Once caught, few animals ever escape. A poisonous bite from the hunter's sharp beak quickly disables them.

FEARSOME BITE

Although their bodies are mainly soft, all cephalopods have a tough beak to poison and slice up their prey. Many squids also have vicious hooks on their tentacles to help them grab onto their victims. The largest beak of all belongs to the giant squid (right). Although smaller, the Humboldt squid (above) is itself a very powerful hunter.

S ome mollusks kill and eat other animals. However, most are potential victims of predators themselves. Some mollusks have evolved ingenious methods of self-protection. Others rely on their shells for safety.

SLOW DEATH

Some of the most unlikely mollusks are predators. Cone shells are marine gastropods that move little faster than the average snail, yet some hunt and kill fish. The secret to their success is their harmless appearance. Rather than chase their prey, they wait for fish to stray into range, then shoot out venom from their harpoonlike mouthparts. Another predatory gastropod is the oyster drill. It bores slowly through the shells of oysters, which cannot escape, taking up to a week to get at the soft flesh inside.

KILLER SNAIL

The Portuguese man-of-war has trailing tentacles that are deadly to fish. But these are no defense against the violet sea snail. Floating in to attack on its raft of bubbles, the snail feeds at leisure on its prey, which can only move with the wind.

STEALTH HUNTER

Although occasionally active by day, most octopuses hunt at night, creeping over the seabed in search of unwary prey.

HELPLESS BARNACLES

The dog whelk eats a wide variety of shellfish, including barnacles. It feeds in one of two ways, either boring through its prey's defenses or sticking its proboscis between the open shells.

STAYING ALIVE

Tough shells thwart most fish and many other animals that would otherwise feed on mollusks. However, some predators have found ways to penetrate these defenses. The oystercatcher, for instance, smashes mussel shells or slices along their hinges with its powerful bill. Shells are no obstacle to the song thrush either. It gets at land snails by breaking their shells against stones.

Often, the best way to avoid danger is to hide. Many filter-feeding bivalves burrow into sand, just sticking their siphons above the surface to feed. The common piddock goes one step further, boring into solid rock to hide itself from predators.

WARNING COLORS

Some sea slugs seem to fear absolutely nothing, crawling slowly over coral reefs in the broad light of day. The reason for their boldness is the array of stinging cells in their skin, which they advertise to potential predators with bright warning colors. A few other mollusks advertise poisonous defenses with bright colors, among them the blue-ringed octopus.

Unusual for gastropods, sea slugs—or nudibranchs—have no shell at all.

STRIPY CAMOUFLAGE

Most sea slugs lack stinging cells and prefer not to be seen. This species, Taylor's sea slug, usually lives among sea grass and is striped to blend in.

BREEDING AND YOUNG

The mollusks are a huge and diverse group and this is reflected in their varied breeding strategies. Some swarm together to breed. Others seek single partners and a few fertilize themselves.

SAFETY IN NUMBERS

Most mollusks produce large numbers of eggs. Many are eaten before they hatch. Young mollusks also face many predators and only a few live long enough to breed themselves.

Most mobile mollusks mate with individual partners, but for those that live fixed to one spot, such as mussels, this is not possible. Instead, they shed their eggs and sperm into the water around them, where they mix together. The fertilized eggs then drift and hatch as plankton.

MASS LAYING

Opalescent squid gather in huge numbers to breed, covering the seabed with their egg cases. Each of these cases contains up to 300 eggs, and a single female may produce 30 of them. After mating, opalescent squid die. Their young take two years to reach adulthood and start the whole cycle again.

MOLLUSK EGGS

The eggs of different mollusks vary. Apple snails, so-called because of their shape, lay large round eggs (left). Many other snails lay their eggs in a gelatinous mass. Giant cuttlefish produce egg cases (above) each containing an embryo that develops into a young before hatching.

PARENTAL CARE

Some species of mollusks brood their eggs and look after their young. By doing this, they increase the chances of their young surviving into adulthood. Mollusks that look after their offspring usually produce fewer of them.

Parental care is less common in mollusks than leaving eggs and young to fend for themselves. However, it does occur in a surprising variety of species. For example, some oysters brood their eggs until they hatch. Other brooders include the argonaut.

Most slugs and snails are hermaphrodites, with individuals having both male and female organs. When a pair mates, each fertilizes the other and afterward both of them can lay eggs. This helps slugs and snails produce new populations extremely quickly and is part of what makes them so successful. Some species can actually self-fertilize. With these, all it takes is one individual animal to start an entirely new population.

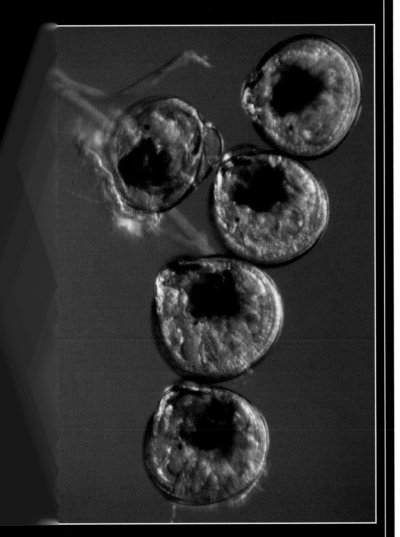

FREE-SWIMMING LARVAE

The larvae of most bivalves and marine gastropods don't look like their parents. Known as veligers, they live as part of the plankton before changing into adult form.

Hanging from a thread of mucus, these great grey slugs are mating. Both will later lay eggs.

SLUGS AND SNAILS

When most people hear the word *mollusk,* they think of a slug or a snail. These creatures are familiar to all of us, since they live everywhere from parks and gardens to prairies and tropical rain forests.

BARE BACK
Most slugs have no obvious shell. In a few species, however, part of the flat shell is visible.

GARDEN ACROBAT
Although they move slowly, slugs and snails can travel almost anywhere. The mucus they use to move helps them stick to plant stems and the undersides of leaves. They can even travel up vertical glass.

SECRET LIVES

Slugs and snails are small, slow-moving, silent creatures. Also, they are most active at night, so they are often overlooked. Yet in many ways, slugs and snails are fascinating animals. They have muscular yet incredibly flexible bodies and most are both male and female at the same time.

In many respects, slugs and snails are very similar to one another. The main difference is their shells. In snails, the shell is external and spiral-shaped. In slugs, the shell has become greatly reduced and, in most species, is completely internal.

PORTABLE SHELTER
Snails can retreat into their shells to escape danger. They can also seal themselves in with a "door" of dried mucus to survive droughts.

Pond snails are closely related to land snails, but unlike them, they have eyes at the base of their tentacles rather than out on stalks. Most species of pond snail feed on algae or water plants, but some eat the dead remains of other animals. Pond snails that feed on algae are popular with aquarists, as they scrape off the green film that builds up on the glass of fish tanks.

Most aquatic mollusks have gills, but the great pond snail has lungs to breathe at the surface.

LEOPARD SLUG

All slugs and snails have a body that is covered by slime. They thrive in damp, humid conditions but shun strong sunlight to avoid drying out.

DIFFERENT DIETS

The vast majority of slugs and snails are herbivores, living on fresh leaves. A few species, however, have more unusual tastes. Europe's great black slug feeds on rotting vegetation and also devours the dead bodies of other slugs. North America's biggest land mollusk, the 8 inches (20 cm) long banana slug, feeds largely on fungi.

Some slugs and snails are actually meat-eaters. New Zealand has no fewer than 38 species of large carnivorous snails known as kauri. They hunt slugs and earthworms.

MARINE GASTROPODS

In terms of species, gastropods are the most numerous of all mollusks. In fact, there are more types of gastropod than there are birds and fish put together.

SEA SNAILS

While land slugs and snails are the best-known gastropods, most members of this group live in the ocean. Marine gastropods with spiral shells are often called sea snails. Although they all look similar, sea snails inhabit a variety of marine environments and feed in different ways. The spire shell, for instance, is a suspension feeder, while periwinkles graze on seaweed.

CONCHS AND COWRIES

These marine gastropods differ from sea snails in the shape of their shells. Cowries have round, shiny shells, often covered with beautiful markings. The entrance to the shell is a slit that runs along the bottom. Many cowries have frilly tentacles that they stick out to find food. Conchs also have slitlike openings in their shells. They have a hard plate, which they can use to seal their shells shut.

PEEK-A-BOO

Like other conchs, the spider conch has eyes on stalks to help it detect food and look out for danger. Here, they are peeping out from its shell.

ABALONE

These marine gastropods have shells that grow in a very shallow spiral. Holes in the shell are used to help get water out of its gills. Some abalone shells can grow to more than 9 inches (23 cm) long. Inside, they are composed of mother-of-pearl.

GILLS ON THE OUTSIDE

Most marine gastropods have gills inside their shells, but sea slugs have no shells and carry their gills on their backs. Like other mollusk gills, these are feathery structures, with several arms further divided into hundreds of tiny "fingers" to increase their surface area.

Sea slug gills are soft and flexible, waving in the slightest current and trailing through the water as their owner moves slowly along.

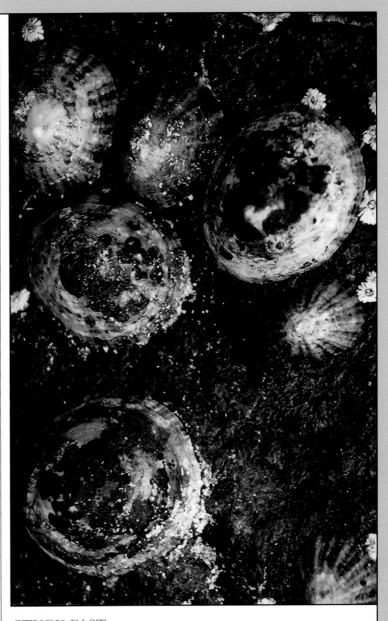

STUCK FAST

A few species of limpets return to the same spot before the tide goes out. Over time, their shells wear a circular groove in the rock, making the already tight fit even tighter.

LIMPETS

Many limpets spend their adult lives in the surf zone along rocky shores. When the tide is in, they graze microscopic algae from the rocks, but as it goes out, some species will return to a favorite spot and clamp themselves to it. Unlike sea snails, limpets have conical shells, which are less likely to be washed off rocks by powerful waves. Like most other gastropods, they feed by scraping with a rasplike radula.

BIVALVES

All bivalves have two shells that are hinged together. These mollusks are filter feeders that use their gills to sift food from the water around them. There are around 15,000 species.

GREAT AND SMALL

Although bivalves all have the same basic body plan, they come in a huge range of shapes and sizes. Some, such as the tiny seed shells, rarely grow to more than $1/16$ of an inch (2 mm) across. Others are truly gigantic—the giant clam can weigh more than 500 pounds (225 kg).

Most bivalves are marine, but some live in freshwater. Apart from slugs and snails and their freshwater relatives, bivalves are the only mollusks to live out of the sea.

SHUT TIGHT
Just before they are exposed at low tide, coastal bivalves, like these mussels, pull their two shells tightly together. This traps water close to their bodies to keep them moist until the tide rises again.

FREE TO MOVE
Scallops are among the few bivalves that can swim, although they spend most of their time lying on the seabed.

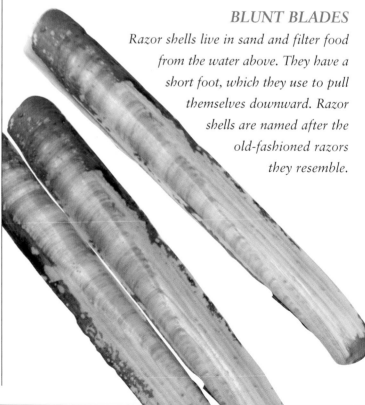

BLUNT BLADES
Razor shells live in sand and filter food from the water above. They have a short foot, which they use to pull themselves downward. Razor shells are named after the old-fashioned razors they resemble.

MANY MINI-MEALS

Bivalves live by filter feeding, straining the water to remove particles of food. They do this with their gills, which are also used for taking in oxygen. Bivalve gills, which are large and featherlike, are contained inside the animal's body. The water that passes over them is sucked in through a flexible tube called a siphon. It is then squirted out through a second siphon, maintaining a constant flow. The particles bivalves eat include plankton—tiny floating animals and algae—as well as dead organic matter.

HARD CASES

Inside their protective twin shells, bivalve bodies are soft and fleshy like other mollusks (above).

STRIPED INVADERS

Zebra mussels are native to Asia, but in the past 150 years they have been accidentally spread to new parts of the world. In North America's Great Lakes, these freshwater bivalves have become a serious pest, smothering and killing off native mussels. They have also caused other problems, clogging up water treatment plants and pipes leading to power stations.

Zebra mussels cling to a native mussel.

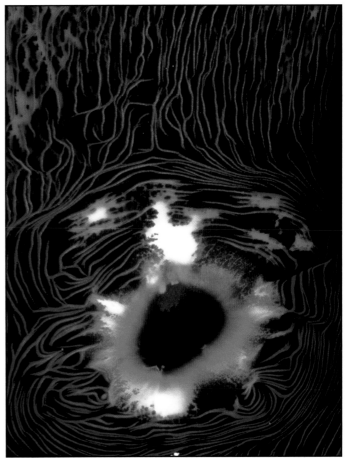

BLOW HOLE

Once water has passed over and through a bivalve's gills, it is forced out of the body through a tubular "siphon" by powerful muscles. The exit siphon of a giant clam is shown above.

Few people realize that octopuses and nautiluses are mollusks. Compared with most invertebrates, octopuses and their relatives are large, complex, and surprisingly intelligent animals.

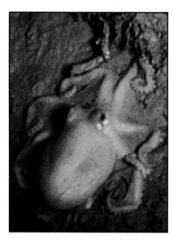

ON THE BOTTOM

Many octopuses hunt by creeping slowly over the seabed, trying to catch their prey unaware.

FIGURE EIGHT
The word *octopus* comes from the ancient Greek word *oktopous*, which literally means "eight-footed." Octopuses do not have feet, but they do have eight tentacles. This is one feature that separates them from the other cephalopods— nautiluses, squid, and cuttlefish. Another is the complete lack of a shell, either internal or external. As a result, octopuses have amazingly flexible bodies, able to squeeze through the tiniest gaps.

BEND AND STRETCH

Octopuses can move in ways other animals would find impossible. Their bodies are so flexible that they can change their shape at will. By day, most octopuses shelter out of sight of predators. Some choose crevices in rocks, but smaller ones may use the discarded shells of other mollusks (right, inset).

CREATING A SMOKE SCREEN

Octopuses, squid, and cuttlefish all produce ink, which they use for protection. If they come under attack, they squirt the ink into the water to cover their getaway. The ink produced by most species is dark brown or black. In the deep sea, however, there are some squid that release ink that glows. This distracts potential predators, allowing the squid to escape into the darkness.

An Indo-Pacific reef octopus squirts out ink to hide its body as it tries to escape.

PORTABLE ARMOR

One mollusk that is an exception to the "no shell" rule is the argonaut, or paper nautilus. Its females produce a paper-thin shell that they carry with their tentacles and use to protect their eggs. True nautiluses have hard, permanent shells. These have several gas-filled chambers, which enable their owners to hang in the water column. Millions of years ago, nautiluses were among the most common creatures in the sea. Today, just a few species survive, most of them living in tropical waters.

OPEN WATER SWIMMER

The body of a nautilus fills the largest chamber of its shell. They have simpler eyes than octopuses, squid, and cuttlefish. They also have more tentacles—up to 90, all without suckers.

SQUID AND CUTTLEFISH

Squid and cuttlefish make up the majority of cephalopod mollusks, both in terms of species and overall numbers. Unlike octopuses and nautiluses, they have 10 arms, two of which are longer than the others and specialized for use in hunting.

STAYING IN SHAPE
Although their arms are completely flexible, both squid and cuttlefish have hard internal structures that maintain the rest of their body shape. Squid have a hollow tubular structure called the pen, which runs from just behind the eyes along the length of the rest of the body. In cuttlefish, a chalky shell, called the cuttlebone, occupies the same position.

Cuttlebones are sometimes washed up on beaches and are sold in pet shops to help birds such as parrots and parakeets keep their beaks sharp.

BIG BODY
Most cuttlefish have arms that are shorter than the rest of the body (above). Their two hunting tentacles are much longer, but when not in use, they are usually tucked away in pouches under their eyes.

GRIPPING STUFF
Squid wrap their arms around prey, holding on with powerful suckers ringed with tiny toothlike structures.

FLEXIBLE KILLERS

All cephalopods are active hunters. Most squid seek their food in open water and are streamlined for chasing fast-moving prey. Cuttlefish have more flattened bodies and prefer to hunt near the bottom, relying on stealth rather than speed.

Both squid and cuttlefish have fins on their bodies, which they ripple to move slowly. To move quickly, they use jet propulsion.

SEA MONSTER

Humboldt squid can grow to an impressive size, with a head and body length of up to 6 feet (1.8 m) and tentacles that are even longer. They spend most of their time at depths of 660 to 2,300 feet (200 to 700 m), where they hunt a variety of fish.

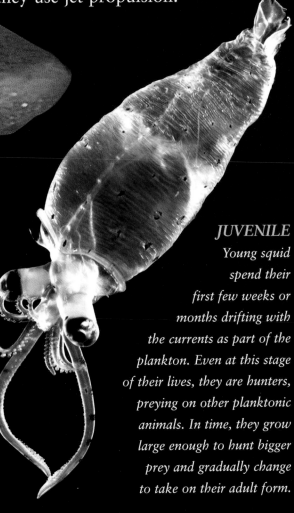

JUVENILE
Young squid spend their first few weeks or months drifting with the currents as part of the plankton. Even at this stage of their lives, they are hunters, preying on other planktonic animals. In time, they grow large enough to hunt bigger prey and gradually change to take on their adult form.

SEA CHAMELEONS

Cuttlefish can change color with incredible speed. They do this by expanding and contracting pigment sacs in their skin. Cuttlefish change color for camouflage and communication, as well as for signaling agression.

By changing color, cuttlefish can match their background to hide from prey.

OTHER MOLLUSKS

Altogether, there are seven different classes of mollusks. Bivalves, gastropods, and cephalopods are familiar to most people, but the members of the other four classes are more mysterious. Some of them are little known even to scientists.

CLASSES APART

The largest of the other four classes contains the chitons. These primitive mollusks have a single large foot, like gastropods, which they use both to move and to stick to rocks and other surfaces. Chitons eat algae, locating it with a sensory organ that extends from the mouth.

The most primitive mollusks of all are the monoplacophs. These creatures look like limpets but have five pairs of gills. Although they have their own class, the majority of species are extinct and known only from fossils, including some with spiral shells.

Tusk shells live on the seabed. They feed by probing the sand with long, thin tentacles. Their shells resemble miniature elephant tusks, hence the name.

Aplacophs are shell-less, wormlike mollusks. Most of the 300 or so species are very small and nearly all live in the deep sea.

EIGHT PLATES

Chitons are marine mollusks without eyes or tentacles. Most chitons are less than 2 inches (5 cm) long, although some may grow up to 1 foot (30 cm) in length. Unlike other mollusks, they have a shell made up of eight separate plates. When attacked, they normally stick fast to the rocks, but if they are removed, they curl up to protect themselves.

ACID ATTACK

Murex are marine gastropods that hunt oysters and other bivalves. Once they have found a victim, they turn the front part of their foot inside out and secrete acidic mucus onto its shell to partly dissolve it. They then bore through the softened casing to get at the flesh inside.

SHIVER ME TIMBERS!

Although it does not look like one, the shipworm is a bivalve mollusk. It lives in submerged timber, which it actually feeds on, boring through the wood like beetle larvae do on land. Shipworms were named centuries ago, when their activities were a serious problem for sailors. Ships and other wooden craft needed constant repairs when the mollusks invaded and destroyed their timbers.

Shipworm shells are tiny and are at one end of the animal. They work like drill bits, cutting through wood (left) and breaking off chunks to feed on.

GIANTS

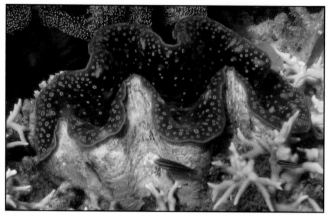

MONSTER BIVALVE

The giant clam lives in the warm waters of the Pacific and Indian oceans. Around 95 percent of its weight is made up of its massive shell.

Most mollusks are small, but a few are enormous. The majority of these giants live in the sea, where the weight of their bodies is supported by water. Among them is the giant squid, the biggest invertebrate on Earth.

HEFTY SHELLS

The biggest mollusks are cephalopods, but there are bivalves that could give them a run for their money. The giant clam, a coral reef dweller, can reach 4 1/2 feet (1.4 m) across and weigh up to 660 pounds (297 kg).

Several species compete for the title of the world's largest gastropod. The best known is the queen conch, which can have a shell 12 inches (30 cm) long. The biggest gastropod on record is an Australian trumpet, which had a shell more than 30 inches (76 cm) in length. Like other trumpets, or tritons, this species feeds on smaller mollusks and echinoderms.

ONE FOOT WONDER

The giant African snail is the world's biggest land-living mollusk. Its shell can be 8 inches (20 cm) long, and its body may stretch to more than a foot (30 cm). The largest giant African snail weighed just over 1 pound (454 g).

This is the world's second-largest octopus. A deepwater species recently trawled up off New Zealand has grown to more than 12 feet (3.6 m) long.

GIANT SQUID

The giant squid is the world's largest known living invertebrate; adults can reach a length of 60 feet (18 m). Giant squid live on fish, which they catch in the deep sea in almost total darkness. Remarkably, they find their prey by sight, using their enormous eyes. Their eyesight may also help them avoid their main predator, the sperm whale.

Very few giant squid have ever been brought to the surface. This juvenile was caught accidentally in the nets of a fishing trawler.

TITANIC TENTACLES

Before fish evolved, cephalopods were some of the biggest creatures on Earth. Today, there are still giants among them. In 2003, the first-ever complete colossal squid was hauled up from the deep. Bearing tentacles armed with fearsome swiveling hooks, it measured 16 feet (4.8 m) long, but it was a juvenile. Scientists think that the adults grow much larger—possibly even larger than the giant squid.

WEIRD AND WONDERFUL

Mollusks exist in a huge range of forms. Some of them are truly bizarre—more like aliens than earthbound creatures. Others are incredibly beautiful, with colors and patterns almost unmatched in the animal kingdom.

ART FOR ART'S SAKE?

The inherent beauty of seashells has been admired by people for centuries. Almost all of these structures are produced by mollusks for protection from predators. Yet despite the fact they all do the same job, they come in a huge variety of shapes, colors, and sizes. Many people find this natural variety fascinating. Some people even build up collections of seashells.

OCEAN GLIDER

The bizarre sea slug Glaucus swallows air to keep it at the surface where it hunts jellyfish. The winglike structures on its sides contain stinging cells for defense.

FLAMINGO TONGUE SNAIL

The bright colors of this coral reef species are actually on living tissue, an extension of the snail's fleshy mantle wrapped over its white shell.

SHAPE CHANGERS

If seashells are beautiful, most people would agree that the creatures inside them are anything but! Mollusk bodies are soft and flexible with no internal skeleton. Many bivalves in particular, look like shapeless lumps of flesh. However, this softness and flexibility has allowed other mollusks to evolve some incredible forms. A few can even change their body shapes at will. The mimic octopus uses this ability to copy other animals and scare away predators. By adjusting the positions of its tentacles, it can make itself look like a sea snake or a venomous lion fish.

Cirrate octopuses have powerful fins on either side of the head that they use to propel themselves along. Some hunt, but this species feeds on plankton, spreading the tissue between its tentacles to form a collecting funnel as it falls through the water.

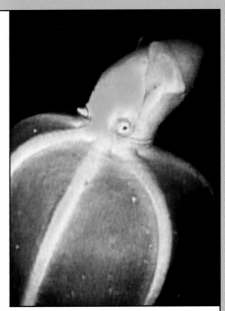

BEAUTIFUL BUT DEADLY

The blue-ringed octopus of Australia is one of the most dangerous creatures in the sea. Although it is tiny, its bite can be fatal, with enough venom to kill a person within half an hour. When it feels threatened, the octopus expands its blue rings as a warning. Fortunately, it is not aggressive and only bites as a last resort.

SEA BUTTERFLIES

These open ocean gastropods swim by flapping the projections on the fronts of their bodies. Some feed on algae, while others are predators.

The bite of a blue-ringed octopus is painless and may go unnoticed until it is too late.

MOLLUSKS AND US

People and mollusks interact far more than most of us realize. Some of these creatures provide us with food. Others are pests, and a few even carry disease.

ON THE MENU

Mention edible mollusks and most people think of the French and snails. However, snails make up only a tiny proportion of the mollusks eaten by humans in a given year. Many shellfish, including mussels, oysters, and clams, are bivalve mollusks. We even eat cephalopods—the calamari on restaurant menus is actually squid.

FISHED AND FARMED

Squid fishing is big business in some parts of the world. Every year, more than 300,000 tons of squid are caught off the coast of Argentina alone.

Although some bivalve shellfish are harvested from the wild, many are now farmed. Farming ensures a controlled supply of shellfish, which means steady profits, making good business sense.

EDIBLE SNAIL

Several snail species can be eaten, but the Roman snail is most popular with chefs. Snails appear on most menus under their French name, escargots.

MARKET PRICES

In the Far East, people prefer their seafood totally fresh. These octopuses are being sold in Japan.

MOLLUSK PRODUCTS

Some of the substances mollusks produce are collected by humans. Cuttlebones (above) are sold for birds to chew on, while pearls (left) are made into jewelry. Pearls are formed by the bodies of oysters and other bivalves around grains of sand that get stuck in their tissue. The biggest pearl ever found was produced by a giant clam and weighs 14 pounds (6.3 kg).

LITTLE PESTS

While some kinds of mollusk are eaten by people, others eat the plants that we grow as food. Slugs and snails are major pests to many crop plants. What they do not destroy, they damage, making it harder for farmers to sell. Their fondness for tender leaves also makes them unpopular with gardeners. Overnight, newly sprouted plants can become riddled with holes.

TOUGH CUSTOMER

Slugs are difficult to get rid of. People who grow plants often use poisonous pellets to kill them, but some of these can affect other wildlife and household pets.

Some freshwater snails put people's lives in danger. These mollusks carry Schistosoma flukes. These are parasites that can infect the blood system and intestine, causing serious illness and, sometimes, death. There are several dangerous species of Schistosoma and many water snails that carry them. Schistosomiasis is the second most serious tropical disease in the world after malaria.

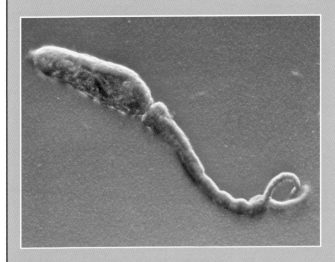

Schistosoma flukes are carried by water snails and cause bilharzia, also called schistosomiasis.

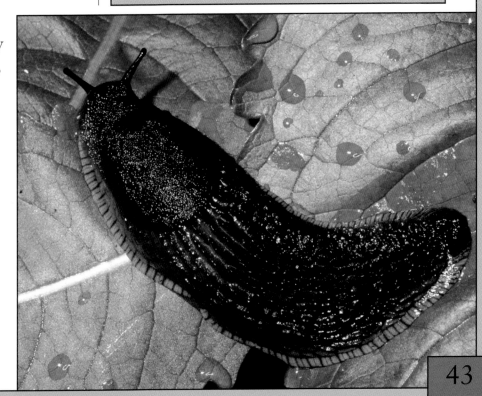

43

ANIMAL CLASSIFICATION

The animal kingdom can be split into two main groups, vertebrates (with a backbone) and invertebrates (without a backbone). From these two main groups, scientists classify, or sort, animals further based on their shared characteristics.

The six main groupings of animals, from the most general to the most specific, are: phylum, class, order, family, genus, and species. This system was created by Carolus Linnaeus.

To see how this system works, follow the example of how human beings are classified in the vertebrate group and how earthworms are classified in the invertebrate group.

ANIMAL KINGDOM

VERTEBRATE

PHYLUM: Chordata

CLASS: Mammals

ORDER: Primates

FAMILY: Hominids

GENUS: *Homo*

SPECIES: *sapiens*

INVERTEBRATE

PHYLUM: Annelida

CLASS: Oligochaeta

ORDER: Haplotaxida

FAMILY: Lumbricidae

GENUS: *Lumbricus*

SPECIES: *terrestris*

ANIMAL PHYLA

There are more than 30 groups of phyla. The nine most common are listed below along with their common name.

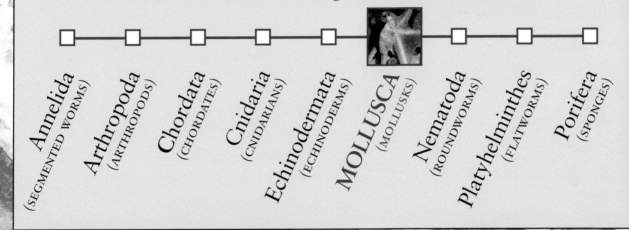

Annelida
(SEGMENTED WORMS)

Arthropoda
(ARTHROPODS)

Chordata
(CHORDATES)

Cnidaria
(CNIDARIANS)

Echinodermata
(ECHINODERMS)

MOLLUSCA
(MOLLUSKS)

Nematoda
(ROUNDWORMS)

Platyhelminthes
(FLATWORMS)

Porifera
(SPONGES)

This book highlights animals from the Mollusca phylum. Follow the example below to learn how scientists classify the *Octopus vulgaris*, or the common octopus.

INVERTEBRATE

PHYLUM: Mollusca

CLASS: Cephalopoda

ORDER: Octopoda

FAMILY: Octopodidae

GENUS: *Octopus*

SPECIES: *vulgaris*

Octopus vulgaris
(common octopus)

GLOSSARY

BIVALVE
A member of the mollusk class Bivalvia. Bivalves have paired, hinged shells and are filter feeders

CAMOUFLAGE
Colors and patterns that help an animal blend in with its surroundings

CARNIVORE
An animal that eats meat

CEPHALOPOD
A member of the mollusk class Cephalopoda; cephalopods include octopuses, squid, cuttlefish, and nautiluses

CLASS
A group of animals with certain features in common; mollusk classes include Gastropoda and Cephalopoda

EVOLUTION
The process by which new animals appear and change over time

EXTERNAL
The areas on the outside

EXTINCT
Died out; once a species has become extinct, it is gone forever

FOSSIL
The preserved remains of ancient animals and plants, or an impression in rock made by the body of an ancient animal or plant

GASTROPOD
A member of the mollusk class Gastropoda Gastropods have both eyes and tentacles; all land mollusks are gastropods

GILLS
Organs used by animals to remove oxygen from water

HABITAT
The area or type of environment in which an animal naturally occurs

INTERNAL
The areas on the inside

INVERTEBRATE
An animal without a backbone or spinal cord; invertebrates include mollusks, insects, and crustaceans

JUVENILE
Not yet adult

LARVA
An animal's young, immature body form before it becomes an adult

MANTLE
The membrane of flesh covering most of a mollusk's body; the shells carried by many mollusks are produced by the mantle

MUCUS
A sticky substance containing water and proteins secreted by most mollusks

PIGMENTS
Colored chemicals in an animal's skin

PLANKTON
Tiny animals and other living organisms that live suspended in water

PREDATOR
An animal that hunts other animals for food

RADULA
The rasping "tongue" of many mollusks

REPRODUCTION
The process by which a new generation of animals is created

SUSPENSION FEEDER
An animal that removes small particles of food from the water

TEMPERATE
The areas immediately north and south of the tropics; the world's temperate regions have warm summers and cool winters

Look for more Animal Kingdom books:

Tree Frogs, Mud Puppies & Other Amphibians
ISBN 0-7565-1249-2

Ant Lions, Wasps & Other Insects
ISBN 0-7565-1250-6

Peacocks, Penguins & Other Birds
ISBN 0-7565-1251-4

Angelfish, Megamouth Sharks & Other Fish
ISBN 0-7565-1252-2

Bats, Blue Whales & Other Mammals
ISBN 0-7565-1249-2

Centipedes, Millipedes, Scorpions & Spiders
ISBN 0-7565-1254-9

Dwarf Geckos, Rattlesnakes & Other Reptiles
ISBN 0-7565-1255-7

Lobsters, Crabs & Other Crustaceans
ISBN 0-7565-1612-9

Starfish, Urchins & Other Echinoderms
ISBN 0-7565-1611-0

Nematodes, Leeches & Other Worms
ISBN 0-7565-1615-3

Sponges, Jellyfish & Other Simple Animals
ISBN 0-7565-1614-5

FURTHER RESOURCES

AT THE LIBRARY
Blaxland, Beth. *Mollusks: Snails, Clams, and Their Relatives.* Philadelphia: Chelsea House Publishers, 2002.

Miller, Ruth. *Mollusks.* Chicago: Raintree, 2005.

Murray, Peter. *Mollusks and Crustaceans.* Chanhassen, Minn: Child's World, 2004.

Richardson, Joy. *Mollusks.* Milwaukee: Gareth Stevens Publishing, 2005.

Townsend, John. *Incredible Mollusks.* Chicago: Heinemann Library, 2005.

Weisblatt, Jayne. *Segmented Worms, Crustaceans and Mollusks.* Detroit: UXL, 2005.

ON THE WEB
For more information on this topic, use FactHound.

1. Go to *www.facthound.com*
2. Type in this book ID: 0756516137
3. Click on the *Fetch It* button.

FactHound will find the best Web sites for you.

INDEX